PET
FROG

by Robin Nelson

first step nonfiction

Lerner Publications Company · Minneapolis

A frog is a small **animal.**

Frogs make good **pets.**

Some frogs live on land.

Some frogs live in water.

Some frogs live in
water and on land.

Some frogs like to
climb trees.

Pet frogs live in a **tank.**

Frogs need a clean tank.

Frogs need food every day.

Frogs like to eat bugs.

Frogs need water to keep
their **skin** wet.

Frogs need places to hide.

Frogs do not like
to be held.

Frogs can live
with other frogs.

We like to watch our frogs.

We like taking care of frogs.

Frogs can be many different colors.

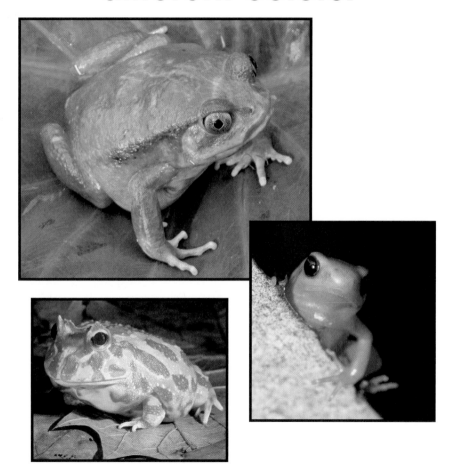

Fun Frog Facts

 A group of frogs is called an army.

 The longest frog jump recorded was 33 feet 5½ inches.

 Frogs drink and breathe through their skin.

 The most brightly colored frogs are poisonous.

 Frogs cannot live in the sea or any salt water.

A frog can change the color of its skin to blend in with its surroundings.

 Frogs swallow their food whole.

 The most poisonous frog on earth is the golden dart frog. The skin of one frog could kill up to 1,000 people.

 Scientists believe that long ago frogs developed jumping legs to avoid being eaten by dinosaurs.

Glossary

 animal – anything alive that is not a plant

 pets – animals that live with people

 skin – the outer covering on human and animal bodies

 tank – a glass box

Index

The photographs in this book are reproduced through the courtesy of: © David A. Northcott/CORBIS, cover, pp. 2, 22 (top); Todd Strand/Independent Picture Service, pp. 3, 4, 5, 7, 8, 9, 10, 11, 12, 13, 14, 15, 19 (bottom right), 22 (second from bottom, bottom); © Papilio/CORBIS, p. 6; © Buddy Mays/CORBIS, p. 16; © Eye Wire Royalty Free, pp. 17, 18 (bottom right), 19 (top left), 19 (middle right), 22 (second from top); © Gallo Images/CORBIS, p. 18 (top left); © Corbis Royalty Free Images, pp. 18 (bottom left), 19 (middle left).

Lerner Publications Company
A division of Lerner Publishing Group
241 First Avenue North
Minneapolis, MN 55401 USA

Website address: www.lernerbooks.com

Library of Congress Cataloging-in-Publication Data

Nelson, Robin, 1971–
    Pet frog / by Robin Nelson.
       p.   cm. — (First step nonfiction)
    Includes index.
    Summary: A simple introduction to frogs and how to care for them as pets.
    ISBN: 0–8225–1271–8 (lib. bdg. : alk. paper)
    1. Frogs as pets—Juvenile literature. [1. Frogs as pets. 2. Pets.] I. Title. II. Series.
SF459.F83 N46 2003
639.3'789—dc21   2001005975

Manufactured in the United States of America
1 2 3 4 5 6 – AM – 08 07 06 05 04 03